BREAKING THE SILENCE
INTERIOR HEALING

Argueta, Blanca Estela
    Breaking the silence: Interior Healing / Blanca Argueta; 1ª ed. -
Buenos Aires: Deauno.com, 2011.
    92 p.; 21 x 15 cm.

    ISBN 978-987-680-012-9

    1. Autoayuda. I. Título.

    CDD 158.1

© 2011, Blanca Argueta
© 2011, Deauno.com (de Elaleph.com S.R.L.)
© 2011, Imagen de tapa Janet Araceli Argueta

contacto@elaleph.com
http://www.elaleph.com

Para comunicarse con el autor: salmista1@comcast.net or
                            mi.nueva.historia@gmail.com

Primera edición en inglés

ISBN 978-987-680-012-9

Hecho el depósito que marca la Ley 11.723

BLANCA ARGUETA

BREAKING THE SILENCE
INTERIOR HEALING

deauno.com

ACKNOWLEDGEMENTS

FIRST OF ALL I thank God, for His mercy and unconditional love towards me.

Father, you know I love you; you are the center of my life. Meeting you has erased all suffering from the past, and having you in the present, keeps my soul from any suffering that could come.

There is no one like you; I could never deny you, because if I did, I would be denying myself. You are the love that I found in the desert. When I was in despair, when the doors closed one by one, I found you. I, who was not looking for You, You yelled at me: "Here I am! Here I am!"

I love you and I will always confess THANK YOU FATHER!

I thank my parents, because they are a fundamental part of my existence. Mom, Dad, thank you. God is pleased because we can walk this part of life together, and because of that I am very thankful for Him. I love you.

And you, brothers: I feel very proud of all the members of the family Hernández Tello. Thank you, I love you.

I thank my family, my two children.

Janet: I love you, you are a blessing. Thank you for being with me at all times. For those endless hours when the support that you gave me made this book a reality.

Tirzo: I love you; you are the blessing that God has given me. I love you because you give me a reason to fight.

And I thank my husband, Tirso: Thank you (I love you) I thank my pastors: Roberto and Elsa Tejada. Thank you for the Church that you lead, because it has blessed us, as well as the members. Thank you for your advice and your time.

Finally, I thank Gisela Calderon Gamio for all the effort and the time devoted to the review of this project. It is a blessing to have met you.

Thank you very much.

BLANCA ARGUETA

FOREWORD

NEVER BEFORE, AS *this moment, have I felt more committed to talk about the topic of sexual abuse. For a long time I have been a witness to the lack of interest towards this situation.*

Sexual abuse victims are people that are still alive. But they are dead inside with countless disabilities and enormous traumas that are often incomprehensible and very difficult to overcome.

Very few want or dare to talk about this subject. Most prefer to ignore it but, this does not change the statistics which grow each day dramatically.

One out of every three women will suffer sexual abuse at some point in their life. This is the sad and cruel reality.

I hope that this book, besides helping victims, will help the civic and religious authorities to be aware of the problem.

According to the statistics, if one out of every three women is abused, this means that at least one out of every three men will be the possible abusers, stalking one of our sisters, aunts and friends. Maybe they will be close to our sons and daughters. It is a subject not to be ignored, but to make a decision and step into action.

If we close our eyes to stop seeing and if we close our ears to stop hearing, unfortunately and as cruel as this sounds, this reality will not change.

If we ignore this subject and look the other way, the only thing that will happen, is more daring in its brutal growth.

We must do something. Assume position and decide for action. Make the determination and the responsibility to contribute to be a part of the Solution. The mere fact that you have this book in your hands is a sign that you will be an active part in the change.

I trust that as you enter these pages, you will find comfort, healing and God's strategies to break any bondage and pain. You and your generation will walk in the victory promised by our Lord Jesus Christ, through the bloodshed of the covenant of the Cross.

As survivors, our labor and responsibilities lie in helping and guiding the victims, to the only One who can help us and makes us free from those traumas.

God is the only one that has the power to heal us completely. Do not waste your time looking where there is nothing.

He heals, makes us free and restores us. We find everything in God.

A Word directed to the pastors:

Sexual abuse is one of the factors and causes of spiritual dryness in human beings. A person with this type of trauma will never be able to bear fruit. Therefore, the help and the comprehension that each one of you may provide them is important to lead them to their total healing.

(Never forget to be merciful).

Now I would like to show you a poem written by a young girl, inspired by a girl that suffered sexual abuse.

REQUEST FOR A GIRL

Walking on the streets, I saw a girl in the afternoon.
She walked with a shocking look in her eyes
that I will never forget.
Her eyes without emotion,
without an illusion for life,
she pretended to be happy.
But in her eyes one could only see sadness.
Despite her fearful and battered soul, she continued walking.
Focused on something else... perhaps something cruel.
Oh! Why was she so quiet?
Everyone passed without seeing her,
but I could not stop looking at her
and I wanted to help her, but I couldn't.
When I wanted to get close she disappears among the people.
A girl only seven years old,
maybe less,
she has stolen my thoughts,
Thinking only in her appearance of defeat,
So unhappy, as if a storm came
and completely took her life away.
Discouraged she walked, as if wanting to die.
She didn't trust me, or anybody else,
Cause' when I wanted to get near her she disappeared.
Finally I saw her again,
I followed her to an alley with no way out.
At last she sat down, and looked at the sky,
Her brown eyes like fine dirt;
Were filled with pure and bluish water.
That her small eyes could not hold,
and it flow from there like a huge river.

Sitting in the dark I watched her from afar,
not to scare her again.

I heard her cry out to the Heavens:
"Help me...! I can't anymore!
This weight is too heavy for me to carry it by myself.
My soul is in pieces.
And my heart cannot stand it anymore,
I live only in sadness,
Could it be that happiness is not for me?"
And she yelled:
"SAVE ME FROM THIS CRUELTY IN WHICH I LIVE!"
She lay down and said one more thing:
"Lord, my desire to live have been taken away by the wind.
In those nights I learned and discover what pain is,
From those nights and those days that I lived,
My life is only to endure,
the wind just left me here with sadness and sorrow that won't let me go
on.
I ask You that tonight when I close my eyes You set me free me from this
nightmare that I am living and never again allow me to wake up to it
again."
As I heard that I could not hold it and I cried.
This child only seven years old gave up living!
So small and has gone through horrible things,
I ran and I hugged her,
And the girl disappeared from my arms.

And I shocked myself as I discovered that the girl that I saw so alone
was Me!
It started to rain...looking at the sky I saw a sign of hope.
The rain comes, it cleanses you,
BREAKING THE SILENCE.

But the wind that comes behind the rain and it tries to tear all in
one strike and it hurts too much.

*Finally the sun comes out, and you find a smile that you thought
you lost forever.*
CAREFUL!
Again comes the wind stronger than ever,
Behind you, ready to eat you again.
Not this time!
I will fight to recover what was stolen.
Courage is in my heart as I remember the request
from the child that lives in me.
That child that is dying inside me...for her I shall fight,
And I will not give up until I achieve my goal.
What child? You asked.
If you look deeply into my eyes you will see her,
and if you keep quiet you will hear her scream,
and with the same request over and over again.
For her I shall go on.
In God's strength.

JANET ARACELI ARGUETA

PERSONAL TESTIMONY

DAY 1

WHEN I TURNED seven years old I had no party, no birthday cake, no birthday song, no gifts, not even a hug from my mother.

I never knew the reason, why my mother was so un-expressive with her feelings, why there was never a kiss, a caress, or a word of love for me. But just the fact that I could feel her next to me, made me feel safe, protected, and with maternal warmth, and that alone erased any reasons that could be in my head.

In the following months I would start my first day of school, and that idea kept all my thoughts busy. What a thrill! For the first time I would have a notebook, a pencil, colored pencils, a book and an eraser. That was the best! I would have new friends, new responsibilities and the same rights as my brothers. I would be out of the house all morning and part of the afternoon, without my mother being worried about my absence.

DAY 2

I felt like a very important and independent person with lots of desires to live!

Eventually the time came, I was overcome by my expectations, if that was what grownups called happiness, I was happy in the full sense of the word.

My first days of classes were exciting and wonderful. I had my first classmates, my first teachers. Everything was new and awesome to me, I was entering into a different stage and I never felt so fulfilled, so free. Of course freedom always bring new challenges to face, that is why when I was coming or going to school I was always surrounded by one of my brothers and many of my classmates.

That day was the exception.

We finished class an hour earlier than the rest of the students. I never until that day, returned home by myself. But the adventure that represented the challenge of returning home alone made me experience a sensation of mixed emotions.

DAY 3

Having to cross the river –with its rushing stream– that was between the school and my house, turn out to be exciting, and at the same time it was also scary. But children are more afraid to miss a new experience than of the dangers of life, so I gather all my courage, put fear aside and I started to walk. With my mind made up, I took firm steps and walked towards my house.

How important I felt! I imagined myself telling my parents about my journey including every single detail, and enjoying ahead of time, the fact that they will feel so proud of me, of my courage.

The rest of the way I walked with an upright face, happy, and that is why, at that moment, I did not see the young man that was in my way. He asked me something that even to this day, as hard as I try to remember, I cannot.

Suddenly the happiness was gone. All of a sudden and violently, this unknown young man started to tear off my clothes until he succeeded and with my eyes filled with tears, I saw, terrified, the wind blowing away my clothes and I was totally helpless...

DAY 4

I have never experienced a sensation of fear in such magnitude. My mind was total confusion. This young man was trying to hurt me in some way but I could not figure it out.

He achieved his goal to remove all my clothes, and after that, suddenly he ran towards the mountain, as if someone was chasing him. He disappeared rapidly from my sight. Completely lost, not understanding a thing, I went after my clothes that were on top of some bushes.

I was not finish putting on my clothes, when I found myself looking at my uncle´s angry face. This uncle was my father´s brother.

Suddenly as I saw him, I experienced a huge shame, and the fear also made itself present. Through lots of violence he made me go back on that road to arrive at a house where one of my father´s sister lived. There, I could see my aunt´s eyes accusing me, as my uncle told her what happened.

DAY 5

I wished that all of the stories that my grandparents told me about the earth opening and swallowing people would have come true at that moment.

It would have been so much better that the earth would have swallowed me, instead of feeling the shame to which I was being exposed.

I never thought that it was possible to have saved so many tears in my eyes. One tear after another rolled out of my eyes without being able to stop.

What came afterwards was a long way home. I cannot tell the amount of punches that I received before being in front of my parents. What I do know is that on that hard, humiliating and painful road to my house, my name was completely changed; I stopped using my name and began calling myself "shame."

For many years that became my identity, the shame, the embarrassment and the pain faithfully walked with me and refused to leave me.

DAY 6

The physical abuse that I took from my uncle was painful, but nothing compared with the pain that I experienced when I stood up in front of my parents judgment.

Explaining what took place to the last detail was one of my father´s demands. He was trying to discover "something else" besides my story. As a method to discover that "something else" he did not stop his physical aggression, such as: hair pulling, punches, kicks and hurtful words full of threats.

I lost all my strength and my energy was reduced. My father's hits added to my uncles' finally send me to the floor.

Once and again I searched through my mother's eyes for a sign of help, but I did not find it.

Here I am! The guilt within my heart and in mind screamed. I just remember repeating in my head over and over: "How bad have I been!" even though I never knew what I did wrong.

DAY 7

Neither did I know if the fear and the shame were normal, but I adopted them without replying. I felt, over and over, that the shame and the fear were rising as a wall that was falling apart, as a threat to come down upon my life to crush me down.

Those same feelings became my best allies to be able to survive. On many occasions the shame and the fear took me to places and to corners far away, so that I did not have to face the reality of my life.

The happy days of my existence were magically gone. Everything changed abruptly, so fast, that I could not yet understand it. My moods were changing: sometimes I cried, others −absorbed in my own thoughts−, I stayed away from reality, from my surroundings. Only sadness, shame, fear and anxiety were present. When anxiety became a part of me I do not know.

DAY 8

It seemed to me that I had no rights in any area of my life. It became normal that my mother fed all of my brothers and forgot about me. I never complained about that, I did not reply nor did I ask for explanations. Today I know that my mother had no intentions of hurting me.

Besides, six brothers and two sisters were too big of a number to know who had eaten and who hadn't. At least it was a good excuse for me to set myself aside.

What I do remember is that when that would happen I walked away without saying a word.

Far from home there was a big rock in a place where people in the neighborhood threw their garbage. It began to be my place. I found refuge there, and I cried there as much as I need it to relieve myself.

I began to feel different from other kids, I could not fit in their games, everything was boring, it didn't matter to me.

My new condition led me to stay away from the group of children and I became a lonely child.

DAY 9

Many times in my need to communicate with others, I talked to plants and to trees; with them I shared my anxieties and my needs, my fears and my pains. They were always willing to listen.

I do not remember receiving any more anger or rejection from my father. My mother kept showing me her love –in her own way– with care and dedication. Regardless of the injustice, I still loved them.

Apparently –with few exceptions– everything seemed to be back to normal.

Suddenly my mother's over protectiveness felt like a fire that melted me down. She wanted to know where and whom I was with and what I did during lunchtime at school, how long it took me to get home.

If I was late she wanted to know why. She wanted to know who my friends were and what we talked about.

DAY 10

It was then that the anxiety made its presence; it grew uncontrollably inside me. I felt that my mother was totally right. I was not worthy of trust and that my behavior left lots to think about. How could she trust me if I had let them down?

Left them down! As a child I could not see what my mistake was and it created so much guilt.

A thousand questions hammered my mind. Why was my behavior wrong? What was my mistake? But I could never find a satisfying answer; I put my questions aside to carry on with a normal life, even though it was only on the outside.

One day, the painful memories refuse to continue. My mind, as a defense mechanism, gathered all those episodes, and filed them in a very deep and dark place inside me, and it raised an impassable wall in my memory, an unbreakable barrier that made them inaccessible.

DAY 11

As much as the memories remained locked deep inside me, what stayed there was the shame, the fear, the guilt, the anguish and the anxiety as inseparable mates that refused to go away.

They remained there stored and hidden as time passed by, at moments diffused, persistent, tenacious and unforgiving.

I arrived at puberty in this condition and next came adolescence. That human stage confused by itself and hard to walk through. To me it became my calvary. Uncertainty came alive in me. I did not know what was happening. My emotions were a tangle of confusion and I began to hate myself to the point of feeling despicable in my own eyes.

Bringing water from the river to perform the house chores was a routine that I had to do every day. As I remember, it was one of the few things that I did with enthusiasm and joy.

One day as many others I went to the river and I met a young man that I knew. I remember that I could not even say hello, because of the shame that lived in me. So, without saying a word and avoiding looking at him, I filled my bucket and got ready to return. As I started to walk, that young man came near me and once again the nightmare from the violent harassment came back to life. He held me, but with my mind made up and all my strength I fought and got out of his hands. I threw all the water from my bucket at him in my attempt to defend myself. I do not know where I got the strength to get away and push him away so hard that it made him stumble and fall down on the rocks near the river. I was scared and started running towards my house, not even looking back to see if the young man rose from the place where he fell and was coming after me.

DAY 12

The only thing I wanted was to be far from that place and return to my house as soon as possible.

I can´t –I feel this is so hard it's unspeakable– explain with words and accurately, everything that went through my mind as I desperately ran.

As I saw my mother, I faked a calm that I did not have, I tried to cover my anxiety and I avoided her as best I could and went directly to my room.

My heart seemed to want to get out of my chest. Exhausted from the effort and the race, I threw myself on my bed trying to think what I would tell my mother, because I had not brought even a drop of water in the bucket from the river. But the question that ate me and moved in circles and more circles in my mind was how I was going to justify myself.

With my eyes glued to the tiles on the roof of the house I made a decision: I would tell my mother and she would understand, or so I thought. I got up immediately, but then fear got to me and I let myself fall on the bed. Anguish was drawn all over my face and the fear that grew as the memories came back; memories that were buried in one of those inside boxes that we all have in us. Boxes that we dare not open because we are afraid of what we might find.

DAY 13

All the memories, one after another, kept coming, almost crashing. I remember the attempt or sexual abuse during my childhood. More than my uncle's beatings, I remember my father's beating, his hurtful words and his threats.

I understood that I could not talk about this with my parents, just because they would not understand what happened, I would probably be treated the same way.

I cried for hours without being able to recover. My world, which seemed normal for a little while, crumbled upon me once again. Never, as that day, had I experienced such loneliness.

I asked myself: "Was it worth it to have eight brothers, a father, a mother, grandparents, and a bunch of relatives? When in reality I was so alone in a situation where I was not responsible at all.

In that moment those feelings of guilt that I had kept inside of me suffered a turn over, I wasn't so sure that I was guilty for what took place five years before.

DAY 14

Confused, disturbed, disoriented, with a thousand questions for which I had no answers, I must have decided to fall asleep to avoid thinking.

There was one dream in particular that disturbed me. I dreamt that I fell in an abyss full of darkness, where I never finished falling. That nightmare woke me up the following day. Then, I was able to remember the events from the day before, to understand my reality. From my reality I could not escape even if I wanted.

What happened the following days was a tremendous persecution.

I had to carry on with my every day responsibilities, which consisted on bringing the water home. There was no choice, I had to walk in front of that young's man house every day, I felt no fear, I felt terror. To be able to do my assignments I created a number of endless roads.

DAY 15

Without considering the fact that it would take twice or thrice the walking distance.

But it was worth it because I never found myself alone with him.

He was my father's friend and he came to our house many times. I ran out to be close to my mother or close to one of my older sisters. It was then that the feeling of hate entered me for the first time.

When everyone in my family where distracted, that young man looked at me from afar and he mockingly laughed at me. That created that feeling inside of me. At the end it wasn't so bad: I felt good hating him.

Hating that man became my only defense. Nothing in this world could make me want to be in another similar situation.

DAY 16

I was next to my mother or next to my older sister all the time. They became, without knowing, the best fortresses in my life. Without their protection I do not know what would have happened to me.

At that time God was only a religion, a myth, something or someone unreachable to me. Nevertheless I thanked God when I graduated from junior high school. My father totally refused to let me carry on with my studies; "Women do not need to study!" were always his words. Even though I didn't share his way of thinking, at that time it seemed the best decision.

I wouldn't have known what to do. How would I face those young guys that have caused me so much damage. At this point in my life any situation or any human being, regardless of the sex, created in me a sensation of fear, and anguish, which I cannot explain with words.

DAY 17

Days passed slowly, it seemed as if time didn't follow its natural course. Every time the afternoon and the night entered I experienced a great relief inside me. Night became my best ally. My thoughts found refugee at night. I also hid in music as well as in my writings. I wrote fiction stories, and happy ones, far away from my reality.

My fifteen birthdays arrived and with it all the young men those were interested in my friendship and —why not say it— starting a formal relationship. Illusions also arrived, natural attraction towards the opposite sex. Normal desires during adolescence.

It seemed as if my life was taking a total turn. It didn´t seem as bad as I thought.

My first formal relationship was very beautiful, until I discovered in his eyes, the same look as in those young men that abused me.

It was a huge disappointment when I discovered that each of the young men that attracted me at first, at the end I always ended up hating them for the same reason.

DAY 18

I could not find even one in which I did not find something similar like laughter, a gesture or a word. Any situation was a reason to compare them and on my part reject them.

It seemed as if those young men were phantoms that were going to follow me all my life.

Resentment and hatred arrived with all its might and when they became allies with my rebellion it created internal damage. I totally rebelled to the established order: my parents, religion, everything. At this point in my life no one had authority over me. I did and I decided without asking permission or advice from no one.

Four more years passed by. But to me it seemed an eternity.

DAY 19

From the age of fifteen to the age of nineteen I turned my house into a jail in which I stayed voluntarily.

My nerves seemed like a time bomb threatening to explode at any moment, my hands shook uncontrollably. In front of people I hid my hands or I used them in some labor so that no one could see that I was out of control.

By this time most of my brothers had formed their own families and this Helped me to have more time alone. I was the youngest of five siblings.

I totally rebelled against my parents' religion. All of it seemed like a charade to me and I refused to follow it. My only religion or the religion that I would follow was the one that would help get out of that situation that overwhelmed me.

DAY 20

One day I woke up and decided to stop feeling guilty about what happened. I woke up with my mind made up to run away from my family and from all the people in our town, who in one way or the other reminded me of my past.

In the United States I found my refuge. I arrived in this country when I was nineteen years old.

In this nation I breathed in peace for the first time after twelve years of anxiety.

For many years I lived with a relative calm. After a while I formed my own family uniting with my husband, who was the only man in which I did not see a trait from the past. I also had a son and a daughter, which became the reason of my existence.

Suddenly my insecurities emerged stronger than ever. My anxiety reappeared stronger than before.

Until one day I ran into the good news of the gospel.

DAY 21

This message of salvation got my attention powerfully, to the point of accepting Christ as my only and sufficient Savior.

I gave in completely to His service. I found myself with a conflict, which crashed against my mind and all of me.

The message of love, hope and mercy, many times came mixed with condemnation and guilt. I refused to feel guilty because I lived with that all my life. And when the messages made me feel guilty, I rejected them with all my strength: "I am not guilty!" I repeated over and over in my mind. "They, the ones that hurt me, are the guilty ones!" I said to myself. With those arguments I defended myself during years denying my healing. The message kept the same, full of condemnation and guilt, mixed with parts of compassion and mercy.

DAY 22

Until one day, desperately, I beg God; "If You want me to forgive show me how, do not blame me, because I am tired of feeling guilty!"

Apparently God did not hear me. Everything was the same. Sometimes I went to Church and it was worse. I even got to think that was the full gospel. I thought that the Gospel consisted in pointing out your shortcomings, your errors and to exhibit you publicly. And many times they laughed at you because they knew your situation, your incapacity, your rebellion, your lack of humbleness and your lack of forgiveness.

Believing that was the full Gospel was not the worst thing that happened to me, it was that I began to preach it, and as I learned it, I preached it. Until one day I felt rejected by the whole church, not because of the messages, but because of my own mistakes. Suddenly I felt even rejected by God Himself.

DAY 23

There was no hope for me; it seemed as if my soul and body would have been transformed into a big empty desert lacking any life.

Once again I experienced the same loneliness that I felt when I was a kid. I cried and I argued with God many times, but I always end it up defeated and asking Him for forgiveness, telling Him that no matter what happened I will continue loving Him. It was that which revealed my guilt, my sin.

Romanos 3-10 says:

"There is none righteous, no, not one".

My whole life had revolved around me. I was always thinking about the sin that others had committed against me. I thought about my own problems, my sufferings, my anguish and my fears. I never stopped to think, not even for a moment of the rest of the people. I did not consider them, their problems and needs, at least not as consciously as I did at that moment.

INTERIOR HEALING

DAY 24

I WAS ABSORBED in my pain and suffering, I thought that I was the only person suffering in this world. I was always centered on myself. It was like me, Me and ME, centered completely in my only world.

Being self-centered has two sides like a coin. On one side people are trapped because they think they deserve everything. They show pride, arrogance, and manipulation. They have high self-esteem and are superior to other human beings, having a very high concept of themselves, even though it is nothing but a front. On the other side –my case– we find people with low esteem that also think that the world moves around them; people full of shame, insecurities and fears. Thus, both sides of self-centered people capture a level of pride that in the eyes of God constitutes a very serious sin.

I never thought that my shame and my fear was nothing more than disguised pride. My spiritual eyes where open through the Word.

DAY 25

The preached Word, taught with love, mercy and compassion, was what brought interior healing.

Isaiah 61 says:

"The Spirit of the Lord Jehovah is upon me; because Jehovah hath anointed me to preach good tidings unto the meek; he hath sent me to bind up the broken-hearted, to proclaim liberty to the captives, and the opening of the prison to them that are bound; to proclaim the year of Jehovah's favor,

"And the day of vengeance of our God; to comfort all that mourn; to appoint unto them that mourn in Zion, to give unto them a garland for ashes, the oil of joy for mourning, the garment of praise for the spirit of heaviness; that they may be called trees of righteousness, the planting of Jehovah, that he may be glorified".

Isaiah 61: *"Became rhema inside of me and destroyed all of Satan's works in which I was captive for so many years and it gave me a complete healing."*

DAY 26

Satan uses our ignorance of the Word as a powerful weapon to destroy us, and from his darkness, he kills us and destroys us.

But Jesus Christ came to give an abundant life.

Isaiah 61 talks about a physical condition, but it also talk about the interior condition of the human being. It talks to us about problems that have affected humanity since man disobeyed His commandment.

The Prophet Isaiah talks to us about brokenhearted people.

The broken hearted. The broken hearted are people that are full of fears, real or unreal. They live with disturbed minds, lacking strength and motivation. Their hearts are burdened with disbelief and loneliness. They are weak, discouraged, suffering from insomnia, depression, despair and oppression.

DAY 27

The psalmist confronted his soul and tried to persuade it; tried to conduct his soul to obedience.

Psalm 42:5 says:

"Why am I discouraged? Why am I restless? I trust you! And I will praise you again because you help me."

Isaiah 53:4 says:

"He suffered and endured great pain for us, but we thought his suffering was punishment from God."

Jesus Christ paid for our broken heart to give us freedom. He suffered in our place. Thanks to Him we do not need to be brokenhearted. His death and resurrection have provided healing for our emotions.

No more hopelessness nor loneliness, because this does not have to be our daily bread.

DAY 28

BROKEN HEARTED

The broken hearted are people whose rights have been broken. God gave us in His Commandments, Decrees and Statutes protection rights in all the areas of our lives. These areas include the physical, the spiritual, the sexual and all aspects in general, and when these rights have been broken this situation is produced. In this condition it is impossible for them to forgive until they accept Jesus Christ, and only when He makes Himself present to heal and to cover all their wounds.

CAPTIVES

The captive ones are the people that have fallen under the power of Satan. They are involved in satanic stuff, witchcraft, occultism and all the ramifications. They are trapped and seduced to all kinds of compulsions and bindings. They are people that do not want to change, who are totally surrendered to their condition.

DAY 29

The Old Testament tells us that the captives of war were put down and the winner put his foot on their necks to show with this action a total domain and control over them.

Psalms 110:1-2 says

"The LORD said to my Lord, "Sit at my right side, until I make your enemies into a footstool for you."

The LORD will let your power reach out from Zion, and you will rule over your enemies."

Isaiah 52:2 says:

"Zion, rise from the dirt! Free yourself from the rope around your neck."

Jesus Christ is not going to come to take Satan's foot away from our neck. He already did that on the Cross at Calvary. We just need to believe, raise and shake the dust from generational curses and remove all bindings from Satan.

DAY 30

PRISIONERS

Prisoners are people who are spiritually blind. Everyday they self-feed on pride and conceit. They live fooling themselves and confused. They are tormented by fear to fail, afraid to lose their castles build in the wind, in their imagination.

Jeremiah 17:9 says:

"The heart is deceitful above all things, and it is exceedingly corrupt: who can know it?"

People trust in their own judgment, even though they might be out of God's will and His Word.

They like to criticize and point out other people's failures, they are vengeful and violent, their minds are always thinking evil against others, it upsets them to see other people's triumphs and recognize the virtues of others.

DAY 31

Romans 12.2 says:

"Don't be like the people of this world, but let God change the way you think. Then you will know how to do everything that is good and pleasing to him."

Ezekiel 11:19-20 says:

"And I will give them one heart, and I will put a new spirit within you; and I will take the stony heart out of their flesh, and will give them a heart of flesh; that they may walk in my statutes, and keep mine ordinances, and do them: and they shall be my people, and I will be their God."

Isaiah 55:8 says:

"For my thoughts are not your thoughts, neither are your ways my ways, saith Jehovah."

DAY 32

What God wants is that we acquire the mind of Christ, that we think as He thinks, and that we bring all our thoughts captive to His obedience.

MOURNING

Mourning people are those who have lost a dear one due to abandonment. People who have been abandoned live all their lives linked mentally to the people that left them. That makes it impossible for the person to carry on with their lives once again. They are also people that have fallen into failure, people that have not been able to achieve what they expected, or they have lost everything trying.

Jesus Christ came to comfort all that mourn. Jesus Christ is the Lord of restitution. In God failure does not exist, he who is in Christ is not familiar with defeat because we are more than conquerors.

DAY 33

Jesus Christ at the Cross at Calvary apparently "failed" but he has taken an enormous multitude to the Kingdom of heaven.

In God's dictionary the word failure does not exist for those who trust Him.

Malachi 4:2 says:

"But unto you that fear my name shall the sun of righteousness arise with healing in its wings; and ye shall go forth, and gambol as calves of the stall."

AFFLICTED

The afflicted ones are people that have been subject to extreme suffering, physically as well as mentally. They are people that are emotionally destroyed, bitter, fearful and anguished.

Psalms 34:17 says:

"The righteous cried, and Jehovah heard, and delivered them out of all their troubles."

DAY 34

In most of the teachings from the Old Testament as well as the New Testament, God spoke and showed interest in the interior of human beings.

HE TAUGTH

For from within, out of the heart of men, evil thoughts proceed.
First clean the glass from the inside.
What comes out of the mouth is what defiles man.
He who believes in Me, from his inside rivers of living water will flow.
From the abundance of the heart speaks the mouth.

Isaiah 1:6 says:

Isaiah 1:6 says:

"From your head to your toes there isn't a healthy spot. Bruises, cuts, and open sores go without care or oil to ease the pain."

DAY 35

In this text, God was focusing and pointing out the internal condition of His people. Here, God referred to their interior, he looks at the condition of men's heart because there is where life is.

His people were hurt and their wounds were not only swollen and infected, they were also rotten. This was a sign that they were never treated, as the text says, disobedience was responsible for this condition.

Sin is the only door through which Satan can hurt human beings in their interior. In the same way that there are an endless number of weapons that men have created "to defend" themselves from other humans. In the same way Satan sets traps to make men fall and to take advantage of them, to destroy them. Sin is his best weapon.

Consequences of sin

Day 36

COMMANDMENTS, DECREES AND statutes tell us about the special care that we should have when dealing with another human being. When we are careless with this ordinances Satan takes advantage and he hurts us.

The damage that Satan does to human beings is of the same relevance. It does not matter if others sin against us or if we sin against them.

Example

If a woman decides to have an abortion not only does she take away the life of a human being, but also a part of her dies. Testimonies say that these women never fully recover until they find Jesus, in Him, once again their integrity is restored.

The punishment for someone who induces an abortion was an eye for an eye, a tooth for a tooth and life for a life.

DAY 37

EXAMPLE

Abuse, no matter what kind, produces hate in the victims towards the Aggressor. That action becomes a sin. But also the aggressor remains bonded to a jail with all kinds of evil, and this will destroy him. His only way out is an encounter with Jesus Christ.

EXAMPLE

The one, who talks about others and raises strife among brothers, automatically enters into one of the seven things that God hates. But also the victims are destroyed with this action.

EXAMPLE

Those who judge others without mercy and without examining correctly, in accordance with God's Word, they will be judgment without mercy, the rod that they measured they shall be measured as well.

DAY 38

EXAMPLE

Based on the subject of this book, which is sexual abuse, we can point out that the abuser shall bring curses upon their children, and these curses

Will follow them generation after generation, and they will not stop until they are destroyed one by one.

EXAMPLE

People that commit adultery sin against their own body. They break the fidelity pact with the other person, causing irreparable damage. However, the adulterer suffers the most damage.

Proverbs 6:32-33 says:

"He that committeth adultery with a woman is void of understanding: He doeth it who would destroy his own soul. Wounds and dishonor shall he get; And his reproach shall not be wiped away."

DAY 39

There is no gain or advantage when we sin. Nor in being revengeful or in hurting others, because when we do it we are only hurting ourselves.

Every time we break God's commandments and sin is committed, the one that hurts and the wounded person both loose.

The Ten Commandments, written in the Bible, show us clearly the heart of God, full of compassion, love and mercy.

The Law was not given to us with the purpose of annoying the lives of human beings, the purpose was to protect, take care and put a wall around you and me. He gave us laws to protect us because He cares about our life and well-being.

God is fair and He would not allow anyone to practice injustice without a consequence.

DAY 40

When God was giving the Commandments His concern was you, but He also cared about others. Therefore, before hurting and judging others, think, react and consider.

Sin is a trap where Satan catches us without considering religion, race or social group. Do not be fooled! Satan is crafty, he has a rope and hunts us. He traps all who are out or acts out of the Word and the will of God.

Satan is an evil being and his nature is falseness, he enters through darkness and ignorance, and from there he steals, kills and destroys us human beings. And as long as we do not recognize him he will continue to lie and to bring ruin with his craftiness.

We must not embrace ignorance to the Word because that is one of the reasons for spiritual death.

SEXUAL ABUSE SYMPTOMS

DAY 41

DURING CENTURIES, SEXUAL abuse has become an aberration and the most powerful weapon that Satan uses to destroy. Through ignorance and shame he has kept victims suffering in silence, victims prefer to suffer rather than exposing themselves, they refuse all kinds or types of help.

Any kind of abuse leaves serious consequences that affect people´s personalities, but in the case of sexual abuse the consequences are even worse.

Symptoms may sometimes be confused with diseases or other type of problems. That is why it is important to pay attention to other and to take care of them as well, even more so if we are their parents. Above all we should always listen to what our children have to say. Rarely do they lie about abuse situations.

DAY 42

SYMPTOM 1

Fears and phobias are the most common symptoms. Fear is developed even from human beings and in a higher degree to the opposite sex, or the gender of the abuser.

All kinds of phobias are developed.

For example we can mention claustrophobia, which is the fear of close places, darkness and storms.

Also all kinds of fears are developed like fear as animals, such as spiders, snakes, rats, etc.

Fears and phobias come with high doses of anxiety and anguish. Actually all symptoms come with these destructive feelings.

DAY 43

Victims are affected in their emotions and feelings, in such a terrible way that words are not enough to explain the trauma with accuracy.

SYMPTOM 2

Another common symptom is enuresis or involuntarily peeing. Normally this happens at night.

This symptom can generate mocking, anger and frustration on the people that surround the victims because they do not understand the situation. This leaves the victims with a lot of pressure and anguish because they cannot control it.

SYMPTOM 3

Another symptom is bad dreams or nightmares.

DAY 44

In my case I dreamt that I fell into a pit full of darkness, and I never finished falling. That terrified me, not just because of the falling sensation, but because the sensation was endless. Anguish and despair from that dream affected me, even after waking up.

SYMPTOM 4

Another common dream is to be barefoot or naked and to feel despair because one cannot be covered. Many times there is a feeling of shame that one experiences during the dream or the nightmare. These nightmares put the victim in a state of anguish, and not only during the dream, they are also affected in real life.

Anguish transcends the dream state of the victim's overstepping into reality affecting the victim long after he or she wakes up. The victim does not know how to shake of that sensation of anguish.

DAY 45

SYMPTOM 5

Another symptom is anorexia Nervosa, which is a rejection of food.

This condition makes victims stop eating food, due to fear they will get fat. We can say that is a phobia to obesity.

SYMPTOM 6

Another symptom is Bulimia Nervosa. This condition manifests itself with a compulsive desire to eat, followed by a feeling of guilt, provoked by fear to obesity. It is normal to find this symptom in people who have been victims of verbal and emotional abuse.

Anorexia tries to take away from the daily diet, all foods rich in fat and calories, to the point of not eating any kind of food at all. Bulimia uses Vomiting as a method to get rid of all the food eaten by the person. Both are disturbances produced by emotional factors, in the root of these evils we find, invariably, lack of love.

DAY 46

SYMPTOM 7

There is another condition that I do not know whether it is worse or not, because I have never heard this condition mentioned in medical terms. I know it affects a large number of people; it does not matter if they are teenagers or adults.

This condition leads victims to restrain from food during the morning, but in the afternoon, it makes them eat compulsively creating a very serious eating disorder.

It is like mixing anorexia and bulimia to make one out of the two. This is manifested by the same fears and phobias towards obesity.

These kinds of symptoms are the result of rejection of their own bodies, originated by the acquired guilt by any kind of abuse, physical abuse, verbal or emotional abuse. The worst is sexual abuse.

DAY 47

This type of rejection, towards their bodies or themselves, is not reasoned or question, the victims learn to accept all that is dictated from their emotions and feelings.

SYMPTOM 8

Another symptom is emotional amnesia. Victims learn to hide their emotions and their good feelings. They get to the point that it is difficult for them to show love and affection towards their beloved ones, parents, brothers and sisters, family and friends. Many of them will never know their true feelings.

SYMPTOM 9

Another symptom is mental amnesia: which manifest itself with memory loss.

Memory loss can be partial and in the worst cases they can suffer total loss.

DAY 48

The mind raises a defense mechanism and takes you into an amnesia state so that the person can survive the trauma generated by the abuse.

In my case, I had a partial memory loss; I just forgot the moments that had to do with the trauma. Memories came back when another similar situation took place. The mind activates these defense mechanisms, and uses them in traumatic moments.

SYMPTOM 10

Another consequence from sexual abuse is suicide. Drug and alcohol consumption at an early age is a common symptom. All kinds of addictions can be generated in the victims.

As an example: porn, masturbation and sex addiction. On the other side people can present a completely opposite symptom such as frigidity. Frigidity consists in the fact that the person does not have a desire to have sexual relations.

DAY 49

SYMPTOM 11

Another symptom is the mutilation of the body.

I have heard very little regarding this symptom. Personally I've never suffered this particular symptom. Maybe that is why I cannot understand it. But I have found it in some victims, especially when destructive feelings come to the surface, as an example: anger, rage, anxiety, fear and impotence. That is when it comes to the surface; people in their anger and despair cut their bodies, like their arms for example to the point of causing damage.

Despair on victims is a huge problem and many times they will feel the same abuser's presence on their bodies. Even without thinking, victims will try by all possible means to get rid of that sensation. In this case they will try to do it through mutilation of their own bodies. In other cultures this reflected cultural, religious and spiritual values, but in this globalize world, They are a part of fashion, of eroticism, nonconformity or identification with a sub-culture.

Day 50

Symptom 12

Another symptom is **evasive behavior**. They do not want to be physically touched by others. They avoid contact with people, mainly with the opposite sex, or the same gender from which they received the abuse.

Shortly, they will try to avoid all contact with other people.

Personally, I avoided all family and all kind of reunions. I isolated myself not only at home, but I got to the point of locking myself in my room. My room had a thin curtain that divided it from the rest of the house. I made all kinds of excuses to stop not only my family, but also anyone that would try to invade my privacy.

Victims create boundaries and they do not give up their
territory for anything in this world, which becomes smaller
and smaller to the point of creating a drowning sensation.

CONSEQUENCES FROM SEXUAL ABUSE

DAY 51

IT IS IMPORTANT to know that most of the symptoms from sexual abuse will appear regardless if the abuse took place in their teenage years or during childhood. The symptoms may continue for the rest of their lives, if they do not receive some kind of help.

Affects from sexual abuse will manifest in all the areas of their lives including physical, emotional, social, spiritual and sexual aspects.

We can say without a doubt that the personality of the victim is affected.

PHYSICAL AREA

In the physical area we find temporary and permanent scars.

The physical wounds that remain after sexual abuse may be temporary, but some may remain for a lifetime.

Day 52

There may be sexually transmitted diseases, such as cases of chlamydia, herpes, syphilis, and in the worst cases HIV or (AIDS) all these diseases can be part of the victim's life through sexual abuse.

EMOTIONAL AREA

Sexually abused victims may experience a terrible lack of emotional control, and this can manifest through destructive feelings such as anger, anxiety, shame, and hatred, tendency to loneliness, fear and anguish.

Emotionally destroyed and confused in many cases, they open doors for spirits of rejection.

This spirit produces rejection and disparagement, apparently without a valid reason. Therefore, victims may hide from everyone, thinking that they will avoid the pain that rejection produces.

Day 53

This spirit will act as a magnet, it will bring upon the victims all possible rejection and disparagement until it destroys them. You can say that it is like persecution that will not stop until it reaches its objective.

That is why it is important that victims get help, otherwise, by themselves, they will never be able to get out from the captivity in which they live.

It may also take them to the opposite side. They can adopt a high self-esteem of themselves. They think they can do anything, that they deserve everything and that no one has the right to tell them what to do, they are self-sufficient. Therefore, they will not admit their dependence on other people much less God. Pride and arrogance can turn into their main strongholds. Therefore, victims will never want to leave that, which has become their protection.

DAY 54

SOCIAL AREA

In the social area victims behave antisocially, not because they want to, but because there is a much-exaggerated fear to rejection. Therefore, they isolate themselves and they have a hard time creating friendly or other kinds of relations. And if they do, these relations do not last long because they do not know how to maintain them.

SPIRITUAL AREA

In the spiritual area, victims have problems believing in God. They have a hard time praying, trusting and establishing an intimate relationship with Him. It is difficult for them to believe in His love and mercy, and they lack these virtues in themselves. They will always feel unworthy of God's love and forgiveness.

And it is difficult to accept and to comprehend His promises of protection and help. They become disbelievers, cynical and in appearance realistic, but below that mask they hide fear to interact with others.

DAY 55

SPIRITUAL AREA

It is necessary to make clear that these symptoms are stronger if the aggressor is the father of the victim.

For them it will difficult to understand how a father, who is supposed to protect and to take care of them, can be responsible for an act of this nature.

SEXUAL AREA

In the sexual area it is hard for the victims to have normal sexual relations, and in the worst scenario they can suffer frigidity.

On the other hand, victims may be trapped in prostitution, sex addiction, homosexualism and lesbianism, which are sexual practices with people of the same sex.

One situation may lead them to another, until the victims are trapped in abominable acts sexually speaking; therefore, victims are exposed to all kinds of sexual deviations.

DAY 56

SEXUAL AREA

We also find exhibitionism in the sexual area. One of the definitions for this word is to show their genitals in public, private or intimate parts of the body. This action of showing themselves nude, in most cases comes from some type of sexual abuse. The use of provocative clothing is another sign. We can also mention in this category the people that dedicate themselves to pornography and to public nudity.

It is necessary to clarify that in the case of provocative clothes, many people use them just to follow fashions and trends in their culture. On these matters you cannot judge lightly, it is always good to be led by the Holy Spirit and let it be Him reveal the situation or the need.

DAY 57

SEXUAL AREA

On the other side of exhibitionism we find victims with an exaggerated need to cover their bodies. The reason is that subconsciously the person has a very strong feeling of guilt and without reasoning they blame themselves for the abuser's acts.

Generally they try to wear baggy clothes especially if they are teenagers.

They also fall into careless hygiene and personal presentation. They will try by all means to not bring attention to themselves.

Victims will try to hide from everyone and will use every method available to achieve it. As an example, when they are children, they are extremely quiet. They can be mistaken as highly educated children. But on the other hand they behave disrespectfully and aggressive. They will try to get attention by all possible means.

DAY 57

INHERITED CURSES

DAY 58

Exodus 34:6-7 says:

"And Jehovah passed by before him, and proclaimed, Jehovah, Jehovah, a God merciful and gracious, slow to anger, and abundant in loving kindness and truth, keeping loving kindness for thousands, forgiving iniquity and transgression and sin; and that will by no means clear the guilty, visiting the iniquity of the fathers upon the children, and upon the children's children, upon the third and upon the fourth generation."

SEXUAL ABUSE IS a curse that we inherit from our ancestors, which through sexual iniquities opened the door for Satan.

With their actions they granted the right of destruction through sexual abuse to their generations up to third and fourth generation.

But it is important to know that Satan cannot cause us any harm if we do not give him rights to do so.

DAY 59

Curses that are passed down from generation to generation are brought to us by our ancestors. Then, if we disobey the sexual norms established by God, we generate more curses and our children inherit them and so on.

It is like a snowball that will not stop, which only gets bigger and bigger. It will only stop when we decide to ask God for forgiveness and break every curse in the name on Jesus.

SOME SEXUAL RULES

1. Do not Fornicate. = "Mind"
2. Do not commit Adultery. = "Mind"
3. Do not have sex with animals.
4. Do not worship false gods.

Worship to false gods is the main door where most of the curses come from.

DAY 60

Sexual abuse curse comes through sexual sins. We can mention some such as adultery, fornication, and bad thoughts sexually speaking. Idolatry also falls into the category of spiritual adultery.

EXAMPLE

2 SAMUEL Chapters 13:

Tamar, daughter of King David, was raped by Amnon her brother, after King David committed adultery with Bathsheba, Uriah´s wife.

EXAMPLE

JUDGES Chapter 19:

La historia del levita al cuál su concubina le fue infiel. Y luego de este hecho, algunos hombres del pueblo de Gabaa, cometieron tal acto de violación, contra ella, que le provocó la muerte.

DAY 61

The Word tells us that God's people fell into these sins, physical adultery as well as spiritual. The consequences were severe.

God given laws are to produce life; therefore, if we break them, it produces pain and death.

As part of the rituals and the worshiping many of the idols mentioned in the Old Testament demanded from their followers, sexual immoral practices.

Therefore, idolatry is one of the main doors where Satan brings upon human beings. These curses will affect generation after generation, and they will follow us until they destroy us. We must stand firm and break them in the name of Jesus.

DAY 62

Isaiah 45.2 says:

"I will go before thee, and make the rough places smooth; I will break in pieces the doors of brass, and cut in sunder the bars of iron."

God promises to break and to annihilate the doors that Satan has used during thousands of years to destroy our lives and our generations.

The Bible says that curses never come without a reason. There is always a reason. The reason for this curse from sexual abuse comes from sexual iniquities.

Exodus 12:23 says:

"For Jehovah will pass through to smite the Egyptians; and when he seeth the blood upon the lintel, and on the two side-posts, Jehovah will pass over the door, and will not suffer the destroyer to come in unto your houses to smite you."

Day 63

We must believe in Christ, believe in His promises of power and authority over the powers of darkness. We must bind them and throw them out of our lives.

We must believe that the blood of Jesus covers us. And that Satan will not have any power over our lives or our generations.

Matthew 16:18 says:

"And I also say unto thee, that thou art Peter, and upon this rock I will build my church; and the gates of Hades shall not prevail against it."

In other words Jesus builds His church in His name and with His power and authority. Satan and his doors of curses cannot impose or triumph over it.

Just believe in Christ and His promises of power and authority to throw out of our lives all the power of darkness.

BROKEN CURSES

DAY 64

Revelation 1:17-18 says:

"Fear not; I am the first and the last, and the Living one; and I was dead, and behold, I am alive for evermore, and I have the keys of death and of Hades."

JESUS GOT THE keys of death and of Hades and He gave them to the Church. The Church has the responsibility to shake the kingdom of darkness and to break every curse and reduce it to nothing.

As children of God, we have the power to bind and to unbind, to confuse and to destroy every principality, all darkness, every curse and any force from Satan. As we learn to detect the kingdom of darkness and its lies, we will break it and we will throw it out of our lives, our minds, our hearts and our houses.

STEPS TO HEALING

DAY 65

AS GOD TAKES His place in our hearts and our will, Satan will have to run; his lies and deceits will be exposed.

Then the power of darkness will disappear, it will completely vanish into thin air.

STEPS TO INNER HEALING
STEP 1

The first step that we must take for our inner healing is to accept that we have an internal problem. Just as we accept and look for help with our physical wounds, in the same way we must accept and look for help for our inner or soul wounds.

Satan is the only one that can hurt our inner being or soul, through traps and sin. Likewise, God is the only One that can heal us internally, through the power and the anointing of the Holy Spirit.

DAY 66

Wounded people have to be willing to surrender completely to God, recognizing their dependency on Him to obtain their healing. Christ wants to heal us, but He won´t do it if we do not ask Him.

Matthew 5:3 says:

"Blessed are the poor in spirit: for theirs is the kingdom of heaven."

To be poor in spirit is to recognize our dependency on God at all times and in every circumstance. It does not matter how hard they can be, God, as our Father wants to get our attention, He wants to be the center, and He wants to be everything in our lives.

STEP 2

The second step for the wounded person is to be willing to face pain and to confront it.

DAY 67

If people do not confront it they will be left in the middle of the road. They refuse to suffer the pain that the healing process produces. Sometimes the pain is produced by traumatic moments that are in their memories.

There is only one way to deal with physical wounds that have been infected. You must take the wound and press it hard without considering the pain that it produces.

If a real healing is wanted, you do not stop squeezing until everything inside, produced by the infection comes out.

Likewise, inner or soul wounds have to go through the door of pain so they can find healing. There is no other way. If we try to hide what hurt us or what affects us, we will never confront it; it will remain there hurting us.

DAY 68

Humanly speaking, we will always try to hide everything that bothers us or makes us uncomfortable, it does not matter whose fault it is. Weather we caused the damage or damage was caused to us.

Pain can also be produced because we remember the people that we refuse to forgive, along with bitterness and destructive emotions left in us by difficult situations.

Matthew 5:4 says:

"Blessed are they that mourn: for they shall be comforted."

STEP 3

In step three in the process to healing, people have to be willing to ask for forgiveness and to forgive every offense or aggression.

DAY 69

Forgiveness is not an alternative, it is a commandment; and therefore we must learn to obey it.

Matthew 6:15 says:

"But if ye forgive not men their trespasses, neither will your Father forgive your trespasses."

Forgiveness is not an emotion, it is a decision. We cannot wait until we feel forgiveness. We have to confess, to declare, to bend all our will, recognizing that we also have disappointed others.

The opposite of forgiveness is revenge. The person that does not forgive enters in a war process against the person has refused to forgive. If that war is not stopped with forgiveness on time, each day it will be relentless, to the point of self destruction, and destruction to other people, with this revenge mechanism.

DAY 70

Ephesians 4:26-27 says:

"Be ye angry, and sin not: let not the sun goes down upon your wrath: neither gives place to the devil."

Do not be overcome by evil. On the contrary, defeat evil by doing good. There is no other way to defeat darkness.

It is important to be willing to forgive and forget all feelings of revenge and to enter into a healing process. To achieve it, you have to surrender in total meekness and to make the decision to forgive, no matter how hard this might be.

Matthew 5:5 says:

"Blessed are the meek: for they shall inherit the earth."

DAY 71

What the Holy Spirit expects is our declaration of forgiveness. If He does not find this willingness in our heart, then, He cannot act on our behalf.

Forgiveness is a benefit for the person that forgives; it is not a requirement or a senseless imposition from God.

Matthew 5:6 says:

"Blessed are they that hunger and thirst after righteousness: For they shall be filled."

After forgiveness, the healing process begins to manifest in a powerful way.

You will be surprised by the hunger and the thirst that will awaken inside you for the presence of God, and to know Him more each time and to do His will.

DAY 72

Then and only then the love of God will flood our whole being without obstruction. We will begin to love God in a way that we have never experienced before, and we will begin to love and to accept ourselves.

Leviticus 19:18 says:

"Thou shalt not take vengeance, nor bear any grudge against the children of thy people; but thou shalt love thy neighbor as thyself: I am Jehovah."

Then Leviticus 19:18 will live inside us without any complication. We will love others no matter how they behave; we will accept them as they are.

No one can love others, if that person does not learn first to accept himself.

DAY 73

Matthew 5:7 says:

"Blessed are the merciful: for they shall obtain mercy."

This is what I have learned from my pastor: mercy is to give another person, not what the person deserves, but what the person needs.

Before healing one can think that the person that hurts does not deserve forgiveness, but after healing you want to share the same mercy; the one received by God.

Never deny anyone this virtue, because you do not know when you will need the same mercy.

Matthew 5:8 says:

"Blessed are the pure in heart: for they shall see God."

DAY 74

Only those with a clean heart will be able to see who God is. The myths and the erroneous images that I had of Him before, will go away from your mind and from your heart. You will see into His eyes and you will be safe.

Matthew 5:9 says:

"Blessed are the peacemakers: for they shall be called Sons of God."

The peacemakers are people that do not only commit themselves to helping with the peace of others, but also they learn to deny themselves, to have an encounter with the peace of God which surpasses all understanding.

This kind of peace cannot be understood with our natural mind, it is only perceived inside, with our heart, in the spirit. This peace which is only given by God puts an end to all internal conflict.

DAY 75

Matthew 5:10 says:

"Blessed are they that have been persecuted for righteousness' sake: for theirs is the kingdom of heaven."

To be able to meet **Matthew 5:10-11** completely; and to be able to keep our healing we have to learn certain rules and commandments that will help us to come out from all persecution.

We must never forget that the transforming and healing power comes totally from God, from the Word and from the Holy Spirit. The only thing that we must surrender is our will.

The persecution that comes from trials many sometimes brings learning and a form a consciousness in human beings. You will never know the damage that you can bring to others until you have experienced the pain that this causes.

DAY 76

There are two ways to learn biblical truths: the first one is through the eyes, that is, through the reading of the Word.

The second is through the ear through teaching.

There are also two ways to obey, the first one is surrendering our will to God, and the second is through the trial or the experience of a difficult moment.

After you have received your healing; you have to enter immediately into a learning process to maintain the victory.

The field that was taken by Satan will be taken by God.

All fortresses have been destroyed, and all that was bound will be unbound. Now God will rule our life totally, we belong to a different Kingdom and we have to learn to live in it.

Day 77

The entrance to the Kingdom of God, like healing, is totally free. It is a gift, obtained through Jesus Christ on the Cross at Mount Calvary.

When we acted and believed in our heart and we confessed with our mouths that Jesus Christ is Lord, we obtained free Access to the Heavenly Kingdom. But to stay inside the Kingdom it is a matter that only concerns you and me.

Likewise, as we learn to live in another city and in another country that is not our own we have to summit to the laws of that place, otherwise we get in trouble.

In the same way is in the Kingdom of heaven only with a big difference; to stay in the Kingdom of Heaven we have the help and the power of the Holy Spirit.

To be established in the Kingdom of Heaven, all your being will have to desire it. Therefore, our joy will be to obey the King.

THE KINGDOM OF HEAVEN

DAY 78

KEY COMMANDMENTS TO maintain our healing.

FEAR OF GOD

We have to learn to honor God, to respect Him as our Father. Recognize Him for Who He is; the All mighty God. We must obey His Word; honor the Son and the Holy Spirit.

Proverbs 8:13 says:

"The fear of Jehovah is to hate evil"

HUMILITY

No one is born humble. We have to learn humility. We have to be aware that God is sovereign, and that he can do with our life as he pleases. We must learn to give Him and others the first fruits, the best. We must put aside everything that has to do with pride and conceit.

DAY 79

Matthew 11:29 says:

"Take my yoke upon you, and learn of me; for I am meek and lowly in heart: and ye shall find rest unto your souls."

Psalms 119:7 says:

"I will give thanks unto thee with uprightness of heart, when I learn thy righteous judgments."

LOVE THE ENEMIES

Loving our enemies is not an option, it is a commandment. But to do it is an act of our will, and therefore, we have to do it, and only after that decision, the Holy Spirit will deposit His love in our hearts.

We must remember that God respects our will even though our will may not be in accordance with His.

DAY 80

Any change in our life depends on our choice, in our will. Regarding our change; God will never do anything against our will.

Matthew 5:44-45 says:

"But I say unto you, love your enemies, and pray for them that persecute you; that ye may be sons of your Father who is in heaven."

DO NOT JUDGE

Our judgment as much as we based it on the Word will always be incomplete; because we will never have one hundred per cent deepness of what we judge.

It is best to leave the last decision in God´s Hands. If we do not do that we take the risk of falling into the same fault we are judging.

DAY 81

SELF-CONTROL

Controlling ourselves is also something that we can learn. And it is achieved surrendering to God, surrendering our rights and summiting them to His Word.

Those who lack self-control will always live defending themselves, justifying, covering and talking endlessly to what others do to them. Those who control themselves will let God´s will prevail.

The day that we enter into a total surrender, everything will come out all right and we will prosper.

Proverbs 16:32 says

"He that is slow to anger is better than the mighty; and he that ruleth his spirit, than he that taketh a city."

DAY 82

MERCY

A merciful heart is the result of the work of the Holy Spirit in our lives. To achieve that fruit the key is to surrender to God in total meekness.

We learn mercy when others reject us, when others judge us, when others criticize us, when others fail us, when others underestimate us, and when others are unfair to us. When all of these experiences make us uncomfortable and make us feel bad, then we will not desire that others go through the same experiences; and through the same pain that we have experienced, then mercy will become part of our nature, it will be embedded in our character.

Jeremiah 30:17 says:

"For I will restore health unto thee, and I will heal thee of thy wounds, saith Jehovah."

DAY 83

Everything that has happened in our lives is the result of our choices and decisions. We have to add the choices and decisions inherited from our ancestors. But it is in us the responsibility to replace a life of curses for a new blessed life in and by God.

Therefore, we cannot expect transformation from God, as if this transformation depended only in His will. He has thoughts of goodness and not of evil for us, and he wants to bless us, to save us, to restore us and to fulfill all His promises. He is only waiting for our decision.

In conclusion, it all depends in our will, in our choices and decisions. But, the healing power, the transforming power and all the power to free comes totally from God.

DAY 84

Deuteronomy 30:19 says:

"This day I call the heavens and the earth as witnesses against you that I have set before you life and death, blessings and curses. Now choose life, so that you and your children may live"

"I call heaven and earth to witness against you this day, that I have set before thee life and death, the blessing and the curse: therefore choose life, that thou mayest live, thou and thy seed; to love Jehovah thy God, to obey

"His voice, and to cleave unto him; for he is thy life, and the length of thy days; that thou mayest dwell in the land which Jehovah sware unto thy fathers, to Abraham, to Isaac, and to Jacob, to give them."

Deuteronomy 30:11-12 says:

"For this commandment which I command thee this day, it is not too hard for thee, neither is it far off. It is not in heaven, that thou shouldest say, who shall go up for us to heaven, and bring it unto us, and make us to hear it, that we may do it?"

DAY 85

The commandments are in direct relation with the behavior that we have toward others. To obey them we have to let go all pride, conceit and selfishness.

At one time, have you stopped to think that we are part of the Body of Christ?

WE ARE HIS EYES

The way you look at others reveals how much God has manifested Himself inside you.

Through God´s eyes we only find love, compassion and mercy for human beings. That is why John 3:16 says: "For God so loved the world, that he gave his only begotten Son to die for us on the Cross.

Isaiah 29:18 says:

"And the eyes of the blind shall see out of obscurity and out of darkness."

DAY 86

When we are going through a time of trial and Satan may appear surrounding us to devour us, we can discern through our spiritual eyes, our enemies are not at all human beings, but the kingdom of darkness.

WE ARE HIS EARS

There are so many complaints that many times we do not stop to examine them. But when God opens your spiritual ears, then you will have the capacity to hear the voice and the cry of the meek, the captives, the prisoners, the mourners, the afflicted, the oppressed, and the ones in jail and of the broken hearted.

You will be able to hear their cry and their complaint, even when they try to hurt you with their words. Even then you will hear, not their hurtful words, but their call for help and need.

DAY 87

WE ARE HIS HANDS

The Lord´s Hands only know how to build, edify, form and restore His children. **Psalms 33:15** says: *"He that fashioneth the hearts of them all, that considereth all their works."*

WE ARE HIS FEET

Our feet only take the good news where there is only evil. They bring light into darkness. They will never get tired nor will they trip over those who trust in Him. They will raise eagle wings. Defeat and failure will fall under our feet. And we will lord over them.

WE ARE HIS IMAGE

His image will be stamped in our character, and nobody will be able, neither to take us away from His hands nor to keep us away from Him.

In Isaiah says: "No weapon formed shall prosper against us."

CHOICES AND FEELINGS

DAY 88

I FEEL THE need to clear some points regarding my testimony and the overall book.

DAY 1

Today, I am only telling my point of view. It is true that my mother did not show much of her feelings towards me, but that does not mean that she did not love me. I was always aware of her dedication and love towards me.

DAY 4

In this day of the sexual abuse story; I did not want to describe it in an awful and grotesque manner as these cases normally are.

DAY 6

On this day, I felt that my mother did not stand up for me, but in reality that was just my view of the moment. Even though my mother did not defend me, now, I am one hundred percent sure of the pain and the helplessness that all of that brought to her life.

DAY 89

DAY 8

My mother never made any differences among her children. To her we were all equally important and we were treated in the same way. If God would grant me another opportunity to live my life –I mention this as an example– I would deny myself if my mother was not with me. I have always loved her.

She has been very important in my life. But now with Christ in my heart, that love will never decrease, but will grow stronger and stronger.

DAY 15

On this day, I chose to let hate enter my heart. He or she who harms is guilty of the damage he or she causes, but the one that receives damage is responsible of accepting the damage in his or her heart. They are also guilty of not taking care of the damage as God tell us to do in His Word. He or she who decides to hate is responsible before God for that sin.

DAY 90

DAY 15

For some, this might sound illogical, because that hate is justifiable. Many times the Word is contrary to logic; therefore I was responsible before God for that choice and for that decision.

DAY 22

On this day, when I tell and mention the term "Complete Gospel," I am not saying that I received a wrong doctrine. With expression I am referring to what takes place when love, mercy and compassion are separated from this message of good news.

For Gospel teachings to be complete and effective, one must never separate those virtues, qualities and attributes.

DAY 91

DAY 22

On this day I am also narrating how I felt. Guilt, disparagement, rejection and the behavior of others towards me have been the story of my feelings. If it was real or not, it is not my place to judge.

I just wanted to tell my experience and the way I felt. We are responsible for our feelings and for our choices, whether they are good or bad.

Therefore –before making a decision– we must always examine all our thoughts and feelings, and check them with the Word and God´s will. We ourselves –with our free will– we decide whether to go to heaven or to walk the road of hell, God is not responsible for our decision. He provided salvation for all and He also provides the necessary help so we can get rid of all our negative thoughts that could come to our mind to torment us.

DAY 92

DAY 24 A 35

Inner healing does not have an established method and never comes by human initiative. On the contrary, it is the result of God´s power and anointing. The established steps on these days are only the most important and fundamental steps, but each case is individual, and we have to be guided by the Holy Spirit.

DAY 36 A 40

The consequences from sin are endless. God will never make innocent the one who is guilty, that is why it is so very important not to have long accounts with God. We must always ask for forgiveness and admit our sin before Him. When we point at others, when we criticize, when we gossip, and when we laugh at the sin of others, we cannot recognize our own sin. Without Jesus' blood, there is none righteous, no, not one.

DAY 93

DAY 41 A 50

Some of the sexual abuse symptoms were taken from my own experience. Other symptoms were taken from the experiences of other women that allowed me to use them. I have been allowed by the Lord to know these women and to minister them in my Christian life. Most of them were abused in their childhood and adolescence.

According to statistics one out of each three women will suffer sexual abuse at one time in their lives. Women are the most vulnerable to this type of attack. One of the consequences from disobeying God was the enmity set by God between Satan and the women, between her descendants and ours and he is doing his part trying to destroy us. Now we only need to do our part, and not only trying but we must destroy him and we must cast him aside from our lives and from our heart which is our house.

DAY 94

DAY 58 A 64

Jesus Christ broke every curse on the Cross at Calvary. And He Himself said "You will know the truth, and the truth will set you free."

We have to know all of God´s promises, the authority we have, and who we are in Christ.

DAY 58 A 64

We also have to recognize our hidden sins, bring them all out to light of Christ. The secret, which, you have never dared to confess, that you do not want to remember because it is dark, perturbing and tormenting. All of that has to come out of the light and you have to ask for forgiveness, so that all curses can be broken.

DAY 65 A 77

At this point I can consider and say. "Walk towards your healing and do not stop."

DECISIONS AND FEELINGS

DAY 95

DAY 65 A 77

BLESSED ARE THE poor in spirit: for theirs is the Kingdom of Heaven.

Every difficult moment and every suffering that comes to our life will always put us at the threshold of decisions. Therefore we have to learn to maintain our choices and decisions within the Word of God.

All gifts come to us from God through the Holy Spirit. This gift has been acquired by Jesus Christ with His suffering, His crucifixion on Mount Calvary. Therefore, He continues asking:

"What do you want Me to do for you? Do you want to be healed?"

In us is the possibility to respond to Him.

ABOUT THE AUTHOR

I WAS BORN in 1963 in a little town in the State of Jalisco, Mexico. My parents were mestizo, part Huichola and part spanish, but I cannot say to which generation I belong, perhaps the fifth or the sixth. I am not familiar either with these cultures.

I lived for nineteen years in that town. Later on I moved to the United States of America, where I started my family; my husband, and my two children: We became Christians in 1993.

From the beginning of my conversion, the Lord called me to His service, I gave myself totally to Him. However, I ran into many obstacles. I understand now that these obstacles were due to my lack of knowledge of the truth of the Word, and therefore of my inner healing.

If you want to write, you can do to my e-mail:
Salmista1@comcast.net
mi.nueva.historia@gmail.com

INDEX

www.ingramcontent.com/pod-product-compliance
Lightning Source LLC
Chambersburg PA
CBHW050551280326
41933CB00011B/1805